kids' cupcakes

hamlyn

An Hachette UK Company
www.hachette.co.uk

First published in Great Britain in 2010 by
Hamlyn, a division of Octopus Publishing Group Ltd
Endeavour House
189 Shaftesbury Avenue
London
WC2H 8JY
www.octopusbooks.co.uk

ISBN 978-0-600-62199-7

A CIP catalogue record for this book is available from the
British Library

Printed and bound in China

10 9 8 7 6 5 4 3 2 1

Both metric and imperial measurements are given for the
recipes. Use one set of measures only, not a mixture of both.

Standard level spoon measures are used in all recipes:
1 tablespoon = one 15 ml spoon
1 teaspoon = one 5 ml spoon

Ovens should be preheated to the specified temperature. If
using a fan-assisted oven, follow the manufacturer's instructions
for adjusting the time and temperature.

Eggs should be medium unless otherwise stated; choose free-
range if possible and preferably organic. The Department of
Health advises that eggs should not be consumed raw. This
book contains some dishes made with raw or lightly cooked
eggs. It is prudent for more vulnerable people, such as
pregnant and nursing mothers, invalids, the elderly, babies
and young children, to avoid uncooked or lightly cooked dishes
made with eggs.

This book includes dishes made with nuts and nut derivatives. It
is advisable for those with known allergic reactions to nuts and
nut derivatives and those who may be potentially vulnerable to
these allergies, such as pregnant and nursing mothers, invalids,
the elderly, babies and children, to avoid dishes made with nuts
and nut oils. It is also prudent to check the labels of preprepared
ingredients for the possible inclusion of nut derivatives.

kids' cupcakes

contents

INTRODUCTION

Baking with even the tiniest of tots may get a little messy at times, but the results are worth it. Instead of giving your children a shop-bought cake, open their young minds to the wonderful variety of textures, smells and tastes of home baking. This book is full of child-friendly ideas for food that you and your little ones can bake together. From Fruity Lunchbox Cupcakes to Pirate Faces and Wiggly Worms, you'll find countless recipes for mini treats.

first baking experiences

Children learn a huge amount from cooking without even realizing it. There's the coordination required to measure out ingredients, to mix, spoon out, beat and spread. Next, weighing and measuring introduce children to the concepts of numbers, weights, volume and accuracy. Lastly, there's the chemistry involved in the baking itself – the transforming effect of heat on food.

The recipes in this book are quick and easy. If using silicone moulds, the cooking experience is even simpler – they are flexible, safe and you can use them again and again. The important thing when cooking with little children is to allow lots of time and not to worry too much about the look of the results! It's the time spent creating something together that's important.

what can your child do?

Because cooking is an activity that uses all of the senses, it absorbs children totally. It gives them a sense of achievement and confidence, as they try new actions by themselves. Children can – and indeed like to – help you in the kitchen from the time they are old enough to stand on a chair and reach the worktop. Covering their hands with yours and letting them think they are cutting butter or spreading icing gives them a huge thrill and costs you nothing but patience. Children develop at different rates, but between the ages of 3 and 6 you'll find that they can stir ingredients in a bowl and, under direction, add ingredients to the bowl. Over-6s will be able to use measuring spoons, measure liquids into a jug and beat ingredients with a whisk or wooden spoon.

basic equipment

Making cupcakes requires only basic equipment. The following items are all you'll need to make a batch of delicious cakes, ready for decorating as simply or creatively as you like.

silicone

Silicone cupcake cases are a safe and simple option for making cupcakes. Silicone is flexible, so it is easy for little hands to use and can be bought in bright colours and novelty shapes. Reusable and dishwasher-proof as well as ovenproof, they can be positioned on a baking sheet for cooking rather than in tin sections. They do not absorb flavour or taint food and they nest nicely together for easy storage. After use, wash and dry thoroughly before storing.

paper cake cases

If you want to experiment with sizes, you can buy all kinds of paper cake cases, ranging from tiny fairy-cake cases to giant-sized muffin ones. Use whichever size

you prefer, though of course if you use a muffin case where a cake case is called for, you won't make as many cakes, and vice versa.

cupcake tins

These vary slightly, but are usually about the size that you'd use for baking individual jam tarts. The sections generally have sloping sides and are also available with a nonstick coating, which is useful if you're making little cakes without paper cases.

muffin trays

These have larger, deeper sections with straighter sides, ideal for making larger cupcakes for adult-sized portions. Muffin trays are also available with a nonstick coating.

cupcake stands

Whether for a birthday party or another special occasion, piling up cupcakes on a tiered stand looks stunning and eliminates the need for cake cutting. These stands are available in easily assembled card or clear acetate, with pillars or separators to create the layers. Metal cupcake stands that incorporate individual sections to support each cupcake are a good choice for smaller gatherings. Look in cook shops or specialist cake-decorating shops, or on the internet, for a variety of design options.

step-up stool

It's worth investing in a child's step-up stool or a child-sized chair so that your child can see above the worktop and/or have a low table that they can work on.

Alternatively, they could sit on a clean floor or on a plastic sheet or tablecloth.

apron

A little apron is a great treat for small cooks. A wipe-clean apron will make it particularly easy to avoid splashes and keep your child clean. A cheaper alternative is to use an old shirt (check out the charity shops) or you could even use a plastic raincoat!

digital weighing scales

These are the easiest type of scales for children to use, as the numbers are clear and easy to read, and it's easier for children to match them exactly to what's given in the recipe book.

small wooden spoon

A child-sized wooden spoon makes beating and mixing much easier for very little ones.

set of measuring spoons

These are useful for accurately measuring ingredients in whole and fractions of teaspoons and tablespoons. Fill the spoons level – a rounded measure could almost double the amount of ingredient required! Don't use everyday spoons, as their designs, depths and shapes vary.

plastic measuring jugs and bowls

Plastic equipment is obviously better than glass for children's use, in case of clumsy hands.

USING SILICONE MOULDS

Most of the recipes in this book can be made with 12 silicone moulds. Cake mixtures rise as they bake, so take care not to overfill the cases or the mixture will fall over the sides and make the sponge deflate. To avoid this, don't fill the cases more than about two-thirds full.

Some recipes make a mixture for more than 12 cakes. If baking more than 12 cakes, or if you have excess mixture and are not using a fan oven, bake in 2 separate batches rather than rotating the trays halfway through cooking as you might with cookies or meringues, because opening the oven halfway through cooking could make the cakes deflate.

Some recipes are better suited to different-sized cases or silicone moulds. You can use larger muffin cases if you prefer, or make in standard-sized cases or silicone moulds, being sure to reduce the cooking time slightly and keep an eye on the cakes throughout baking.

It's not always necessary to use baking sheets with silicone moulds, but they do support the paper cases particularly well. Pages 7–9 list some of the other equipment that may come in useful.

safety first

Small children must always be supervised in the kitchen. Teach them basic hygiene rules from an early age, as well as telling them about the potential dangers posed by hot ovens, full saucepans and sharp knives.

hygiene

Always wash hands before starting to cook and make sure surfaces are clean. Tie back long hair and wear an apron or coverall.

ovens and hobs

Take special care when opening oven doors in front of young cooks and make sure they stand well back so they don't get blasted by hot air. Always use oven gloves. Be especially wary of recently turned-off but still very hot hobs. Use the back rings of the hob when working with small children so they are not tempted to grab saucepan handles from below to see what's cooking.

sharp knives

It's great to involve young children in the clearing-up process, but it is important to make it a rule never to place any sharp knives or food processor blades in the sink, where they can easily be hidden by soap bubbles. Instead, wash them as you go and place knives straight back on a knife rack or in a drawer, and processor blades in their storage box, well out of harm's way.

some simple techniques

Unlike larger cakes, which are more prone to sinking in the centre or being over- or undercooked, there's less that can go wrong when making cupcakes.

mixing the basic sponge

Some of the recipes use the 'all-in-one' method, in which all the cake ingredients are beaten together in a bowl using a hand-held electric whisk or a wooden spoon. Make sure you've softened the butter beforehand so that the mixture creams together easily. This will take about 1 minute using the whisk or 3–4 minutes if you're using a wooden spoon. An alternative, more traditional, method is to cream the butter and sugar, beat in the eggs, then sift in the flour and gently fold it in, sometimes adding a little liquid so that the mixture forms a dropping consistency. Both methods can also be used in a free-standing electric mixer or a large food processor.

making muffins

Muffins are made by folding the 'wet' ingredients, such as eggs, melted butter and buttermilk or milk, into the dry ingredients, including the flour, baking powder, dried fruits and flavourings. Use a large metal spoon and fold the ingredients gently together until they're only just combined: overmixing the ingredients will produce a tougher texture. It doesn't matter if there are traces of flour dispersed in the mixture.

out of the oven, then carefully lift them on to a wire rack. Leave until completely cold before decorating, particularly if using whipped cream or buttercream. Muffins don't keep well and any leftovers should be warmed through to refresh them before serving. Ideally, any that are not eaten freshly baked should be frozen for later use.

storing cupcakes

Cupcakes are best served freshly baked. However, if you are making them ahead, they'll keep well in an airtight container for 24 hours. If you are keeping them for more than a couple of days, it's best to freeze them, allowing them to thaw for several hours before decorating. Cakes decorated with buttercream or chocolate frosting can be frozen ready decorated, but those finished with whipped cream or icings are best decorated once thawed.

piping decorations

Ingredients such as whipped cream, meringue, melted chocolate and buttercream can be piped on to cupcakes for a more formal, uniform presentation rather than simply being spooned or spread with a knife. Reusable nylon piping bags, available from specialist cake-decorating shops or cook shops, can be fitted with a star or plain piping nozzle for piping and then washed ready for reuse.

If you are piping scribbled lines or more intricate decorations, a paper piping bag is an easier option. These can be bought ready made from good cake-decorating suppliers or you can make your own from triangles of greaseproof paper. The advantage of using a disposable

testing whether the cakes are cooked

At the end of the cooking time, gently open the oven and lightly touch the top of 1 of the cakes. The cakes should have risen and the surface should feel soft but still firm to the touch. For a basic sponge mixture the crust should be pale golden. Avoid overcooking or the cakes will taste dry.

cooling the cakes

Most of the cupcakes are cooled before decorating. Leave them for a couple of minutes once you have taken them bag is that you can have several different bags in use at one time, for example when using different-coloured icings for decoration. It also means that you can snip off the merest tip of the bag for piping without having to insert a plastic or metal nozzle. Take care not to snip off too much of the tip or the icing will flow out too thick and fast.

making a paper piping bag

Cut out a 25 cm (10 inch) square of greaseproof paper. Fold it diagonally in half. Cut the paper in half, just to one side of the folded line. Holding 1 piece with the long edge

away from you, curl the right-hand point over to meet the centre point, making a cone shape. Bring the left-hand point over the cone so the 3 points meet. Fold the points over several times to secure the cone. Snip off the tip and insert a piping nozzle, if using. Half fill the bag with icing and fold over the end to secure.

using writing icing

Tubes of writing icing can be bought in many colours. Some come with changeable tips for piping.

melting chocolate

To melt on the hob, chop the chocolate into small pieces and put in a heatproof bowl. Set the bowl over a saucepan of gently simmering water, making sure the base of the bowl doesn't come in contact with the water. Once the chocolate starts to melt, turn off the heat and leave until completely melted, stirring once or twice until no lumps remain. It's crucial that no water (including steam) gets into the bowl or the chocolate will solidify and cannot be melted again.

To melt in a microwave oven, chop the chocolate into small pieces and put in a microwave-proof bowl. Melt the chocolate in one-minute spurts, checking frequently. Take particular care when melting white or milk chocolate, as they have a higher sugar content and are more prone to scorching.

To melt in the oven, chop the chocolate into small pieces and place in an ovenproof dish or bowl. Put in the switched-off oven after baking and leave until melted.

using ready-to-roll icing

This soft, pliable icing is available from supermarkets, usually in white or basic colours, or in a wider range of colours from specialist cake-decorating shops or suppliers. It can be rolled out on a surface lightly dusted with icing sugar and cut into shapes using cutters or moulded like Plasticine into shapes. If opening a new slab of ready-to-roll icing, knead it lightly to soften it up before rolling out. White icing can be coloured by kneading in a few drops of liquid food colouring (to a pastel shade) or paste colouring (for a stronger shade). Any icing that's not in use should be wrapped tightly in clingfilm to prevent it drying out.

using ready-made decorations

These decorations can range from supermarket-bought sugar sprinkles, tiny sweets and chocolates through to handmade edible flowers available from specialist cake-decorating shops or suppliers. You may want to check the ingredients used in some of the cheaper bought decorations before you decide to buy them, or at least use them very sparingly.

fillings and toppings

The following favourite fillings and toppings are used in the book and can also be used for other cupcake recipes of your choice. All 3 recipes are quick and easy to make, but the frostings take a little longer than the buttercream, as the chocolate needs to be melted.

buttercream

MAKES ENOUGH TO COVER 12 CUPCAKES

PREPARATION TIME 5 MINUTES

150 g (5 oz) unsalted butter, softened
250 g (8 oz) icing sugar, sifted
1 teaspoon vanilla extract
2 teaspoons hot water

Put the butter and icing sugar in a bowl and beat well with a wooden spoon or hand-held electric whisk until smooth and creamy. Add the vanilla extract and hot water and beat again until smooth.

chocolate fudge frosting

MAKES ENOUGH TO COVER 12 CUPCAKES

PREPARATION TIME 5 MINUTES

COOKING TIME 5 MINUTES

100 g (3½ oz) plain chocolate or milk chocolate, chopped
2 tablespoons milk
50 g (2 oz) unsalted butter
75 g (3 oz) icing sugar, sifted

Put the chocolate, milk and butter in a small, heavy-based saucepan and heat gently, stirring, until the chocolate and butter have melted.

Remove from the heat and stir in the icing sugar until smooth. Spread the frosting over the tops of cupcakes while still warm.

white chocolate fudge frosting

MAKES ENOUGH TO COVER 12 CUPCAKES

PREPARATION TIME 5 MINUTES

COOKING TIME 5 MINUTES

200 g (7 oz) white chocolate, chopped
5 tablespoons milk
175 g (6 oz) icing sugar, sifted

Melt the chocolate and milk in a heatproof bowl. Set the bowl over a saucepan of very gently simmering water and leave until melted, stirring frequently.

Remove the bowl from the pan and stir in the icing sugar until smooth. Spread the frosting over the tops of cupcakes while still warm.

vanilla cupcakes

MAKES 12

PREPARATION TIME 10 MINUTES

COOKING TIME 20 MINUTES

150 g (5 oz) butter, softened
150 g (5 oz) caster sugar
175 g (6 oz) self-raising flour, sifted
3 eggs
1 teaspoon vanilla extract

1 Stand 12 silicone cupcake cases on a baking sheet or line a 12-section cupcake tin with paper or foil cake cases.

2 Put all the cake ingredients in a bowl and beat with a hand-held electric whisk or a wooden spoon until light and creamy. Divide the cake mixture between the cases.

3 Bake in a preheated oven, 180°C (350°F), Gas Mark 4, for 20 minutes or until risen and just firm to the touch. Transfer to a wire rack to cool.

rainbow cupcakes

MAKES 12

PREPARATION TIME 20 MINUTES

COOKING TIME 10–15 MINUTES

50 g (2 oz) butter, softened
50 g (2 oz) caster sugar
grated rind of 1 orange
a few drops of vanilla extract
1 egg
50 g (2 oz) self-raising flour, sifted

FOR THE ICING AND DECORATION

175 g (6 oz) icing sugar, sifted
2 tablespoons orange juice
hundreds and thousands or other cake
    decorations

1 Stand 12 silicone cupcake cases on a baking sheet or line a 12-section cupcake tin with paper or foil cake cases.

2 Put the butter, caster sugar, orange rind and vanilla extract in a bowl and beat with a hand-held electric whisk or wooden spoon until light and creamy. Add the egg and beat the mixture again, then add the flour and gently fold it in with a large metal spoon. Divide the cake mixture between the cases.

3 Bake in a preheated oven, 180°C (350°F), Gas Mark 4, for 10–15 minutes or until they are risen and golden. Remove from the oven and allow to cool for a few minutes before transferring to a wire rack to cool completely.

4 Meanwhile, make the icing by stirring the icing sugar and orange juice together in a bowl.

5 Drizzle the icing over the cooled cakes with a teaspoon or dip them into the icing to cover. Pour the hundreds and thousands into a saucer and dip the iced cakes into them. Leave to set.

funny faces

MAKES 12

PREPARATION TIME 20 MINUTES

COOKING TIME 20 MINUTES

100 g (3½ oz) butter, softened
100 g (3½ oz) caster sugar
2 eggs
100 g (3½ oz) self-raising flour
3 tablespoons cocoa powder

FOR THE BUTTERCREAM AND DECORATION
75 g (3 oz) butter, softened
175 g (6 oz) icing sugar, sifted
1 tablespoon milk or water
2–3 drops of red food colouring
2 tablespoons cocoa powder, sifted
icing pens
white chocolate buttons and milk chocolate
   buttons
cake decorations

1 Stand 12 silicone cupcake cases on a baking sheet or line a 12-section cupcake tin with paper or foil cake cases.

2 Put the butter and caster sugar in a bowl and beat with a hand-held electric whisk or wooden spoon until light and creamy. Add the eggs, beating after each addition. Sift in the flour and cocoa powder and gently fold them in with a large metal spoon. Divide the cake mixture between the cases.

3 Bake in a preheated oven, 180°C (350°F), Gas Mark 4, for 20 minutes or until risen and just firm to the touch.

4 Leave to cool in the tin for a few minutes, then transfer to a wire rack to cool completely.

5 Meanwhile, make the buttercream. Put the butter, icing sugar and milk in a bowl and beat with a hand-held electric whisk or wooden spoon until light and creamy. Divide the buttercream into 2 bowls. Add the colouring to one and the cocoa powder to the other and mix well. Leave in a cool place.

6 Smooth the buttercream on top of the cooled cakes with the back of a teaspoon, then use your imagination to decorate them with lots of different funny faces.

frosted banana cupcakes

MAKES 12

PREPARATION TIME 25 MINUTES,
  PLUS COOLING

COOKING TIME 20 MINUTES

100 g (3½ oz) butter, softened
100 g (3½ oz) golden caster sugar
2 eggs
125 g (4 oz) self-raising flour
½ teaspoon baking powder
1 ripe banana, mashed
75 g (3 oz) sultanas

FOR THE ICING AND DECORATION
100 g (3½ oz) Greek yogurt
250 g (8 oz) golden icing sugar, sifted
sugar sprinkles, to decorate

1 Stand 12 silicone cupcake cases on a baking sheet or line a 12-section cupcake tin with paper or foil cake cases.

2 Put the butter, caster sugar and eggs in a bowl, sift in the flour and baking powder and beat with a hand-held electric whisk or a wooden spoon until light and creamy. Stir in the mashed banana and the sultanas. Divide the cake mixture between the cases.

3 Bake in a preheated oven, 180°C (350°F), Gas Mark 4, for 20 minutes or until risen and just firm to the touch. Transfer to a wire rack to cool.

4 Line a bowl with a double thickness of kitchen paper. Spoon the yogurt on to the paper. Bring up the edges and gently squeeze out as much liquid as possible. Tip the thickened ball of yogurt onto 2 more sheets of kitchen paper and squeeze out a little more liquid if possible.

5 Put the icing sugar into a separate bowl and add the thick yogurt. Mix well to make an icing with a slightly fudgy texture. Swirl the mixture over the cakes and scatter with sugar sprinkles to decorate.

chocolate teddies

MAKES 12

PREPARATION TIME 20 MINUTES

COOKING TIME 10–15 MINUTES

100 g (3½ oz) butter, softened
100 g (3½ oz) caster sugar
a few drops of vanilla extract
2 eggs
100 g (3½ oz) self-raising flour, sifted
50 g (2 oz) milk chocolate drops, plus
    extra to decorate
50 g (2 oz) white chocolate drops, plus
    extra to decorate

FOR THE BUTTERCREAM

150 g (5 oz) icing sugar
2 tablespoons cocoa powder
50 g (2 oz) butter, softened

1 Stand 12 silicone cupcake cases on a baking sheet or line a 12-section cupcake tin with paper or foil cake cases.

2 Put the butter, caster sugar and vanilla extract in a bowl and beat with a hand-held electric whisk or a wooden spoon until light and creamy. Add the eggs, beating after each addition, then add the flour and gently fold it in with a large metal spoon. Finally, stir in the chocolate drops. Divide the cake mixture between the cases.

3 Bake in a preheated oven, 180°C (350°F), Gas Mark 4, for 10–15 minutes or until risen and just firm to the touch. Leave to cool in the tin for a few minutes before transferring to a wire rack to cool completely.

4 Meanwhile, make the chocolate buttercream by sifting the icing sugar and cocoa into a bowl, adding the butter, then beating the ingredients together with a hand-held electric whisk or a wooden spoon until smooth.

5 Spread the buttercream over the cooled cakes. Use a fork to make the buttercream look like fur, then decorate the cakes using the remaining chocolate drops to make eyes, ears and a nose.

fruity lunchbox cupcakes

MAKES 12

PREPARATION TIME 10 MINUTES

COOKING TIME 15 MINUTES

100 g (3½ oz) plain flour
100 g (3½ oz) wholemeal flour
2 teaspoons baking powder
75 g (3 oz) golden caster sugar
2 eggs
2 tablespoons mild olive oil or vegetable oil
40 g (1½ oz) butter, melted
2 teaspoons vanilla extract
150 g (5 oz) red fruit yogurt, such as strawberry,
   raspberry or cherry
100 g (½ oz) raspberries or strawberries, cut into
   small pieces

1 Stand 12 silicone cupcake cases on a baking sheet or line a 12-section cupcake tin with paper or foil cake cases.

2 Sift the flours and baking powder into a bowl, adding the bran from the sieve. Add the caster sugar. Whisk together the eggs, oil, melted butter, vanilla extract and yogurt with a fork in a jug and add to the bowl. Mix gently with a large metal spoon until the ingredients have started to blend together.

3 Scatter with half the berry pieces and mix a little more until the ingredients are only just combined. Divide the cake mixture between the cases. Scatter with the remaining berry pieces.

4 Bake in a preheated oven, 200°C (400°F), Gas Mark 6, for 15 minutes or until well risen and just firm to the touch. Transfer to a wire rack to cool.

butterfly cakes

MAKES 12

PREPARATION TIME 20 MINUTES

COOKING TIME 20 MINUTES

100 g (3½ oz) butter, softened
100 g (3½ oz) caster sugar
2 drops of vanilla extract
2 eggs
100 g (3½ oz) self-raising flour, sifted

FOR THE BUTTERCREAM AND DECORATION

50 g (2 oz) butter, softened
125 g (4 oz) icing sugar, sifted, plus extra
   for dusting
2–3 drops of food colouring (optional)
1 tablespoon milk or water
icing pens, to decorate (optional)

1 Stand 12 silicone cupcake cases on a baking sheet or line a 12-section cupcake tin with paper or foil cake cases.

2 Put the butter, caster sugar and vanilla extract in a bowl and beat with a hand-held electric whisk or a wooden spoon until light and creamy. Add the eggs, beating after each addition, then add the flour and gently fold it in with a large metal spoon. Divide the cake mixture between the cases.

3 Bake in a preheated oven, 180°C (350°F), Gas Mark 4, for 20 minutes or until risen and just firm to the touch. Leave to cool in the tin for a few minutes before transferring to a wire rack to cool completely.

4 Meanwhile, make the buttercream. Place all the ingredients in a bowl and beat together until light and creamy.

5 Use a teaspoon to dig out a circle about 2.5 cm (1 inch) in diameter from the top of each cake. Slice the cone-like piece of cake you have dug out in half.

6 Fill the holes in the cakes with the buttercream, then stick the 2 halves of each cone back into the icing so that they stick up like a butterfly perched on top. Dust with icing sugar and/or decorate with icing pens, if wanted.

wiggly worms

MAKES 12

PREPARATION TIME 45 MINUTES,
  PLUS COOLING

COOKING TIME 20 MINUTES

75 g (3 oz) unsalted butter, softened
125 g (4 oz) icing sugar, sifted, plus extra
  for dusting
12 Vanilla Cupcakes (see page 16)
50 g (2 oz) milk chocolate, grated
100 g (2 oz) pink ready-to-roll icing or red
  ready-to-roll icing
50 g (3½ oz) chocolate-flavoured ready-
  to-roll icing
12 small candy-covered chocolate sweets

1 Put the butter and sugar in a bowl and beat with a hand-held electric whisk or a wooden spoon until light and creamy. Remove 1 cooled cake from its case and take a thick, angled slice off the top. Spread a little of the buttercream over another cake, position the slice on top and spread with a little more buttercream to make a larger 'face' cake.

2 Spread a large, rectangular cake board with 4 tablespoons of the buttercream and scatter with the grated chocolate. Spread the remaining buttercream over the cakes, then position in a snaking line over the chocolate with the face cake at the front.

3 Roll out the coloured icing thinly on a worktop lightly dusted with icing sugar and cut out 9 rounds using a 5 cm (2 inch) cookie cutter. Place on all the cakes except the face and end cakes. Cut out a pointed tail from the trimmings and place on the end cake. Roll out the chocolate icing and cut out a slightly larger round. Position on the front cake.

4 Roll out the chocolate icing thinly and cut out 2.5 cm (1 inch) rounds. Place on the rest of the cakes and top each with a candy-covered chocolate sweet. Shape and position the eyes and mouth using icing trimmings and the 2 remaining sweets.

flower fairy cakes

MAKES 12

PREPARATION TIME 10 MINUTES

COOKING TIME 15–20 MINUTES

125 g (4 oz) butter, softened
125 g (4 oz) caster sugar
2 eggs
125 g (4 oz) self-raising flour, sifted
a few drops of vanilla extract
2 tablespoons milk

FOR THE ICING AND DECORATION
500 g (1 lb) pack instant royal icing
food colouring (one or more colours, as desired)
sugar flowers or rice paper flowers or other
    cake decorations

1 Stand 12 silicone cupcake cases on a baking sheet or line a 12-section cupcake tin with paper or foil cake cases.

2 Put all the cake ingredients, except for the milk, into a bowl and beat with a hand-held electric whisk or a wooden spoon until light and creamy. Add the milk a little at a time while beating until you have a mixture that is a soft, dropping consistency. Divide the cake mixture between the cases.

3 Bake in a preheated oven, 180°C (350°F), Gas Mark 4, for 15–20 minutes or until risen and just firm to the touch. Leave to cool in the tin for a few minutes, then transfer to a wire rack. When cool, slice off the pointy tops with a sharp knife.

4 Make up the royal icing as directed on the pack, then divide into small bowls, 1 for each choice of colour. Add drops of the chosen colour(s), and mix, until you achieve the colour(s) your want. Spoon the icing on to the cakes and decorate.

warm chocolate brownie cupcakes

MAKES ABOUT 18

PREPARATION TIME 10 MINUTES

COOKING TIME 12 MINUTES

200 g (7 oz) plain chocolate, chopped
150 g (5 oz) butter
3 eggs
200 g (7 oz) light muscovado sugar
125 g (4 oz) self-raising flour
½ teaspoon baking powder
100 g (3½ oz) milk chocolate, chopped finely
100 g (3½ oz) pecan nuts or walnuts, finely
   chopped
cocoa powder, sifted, for dusting (optional)
ice cream, to serve

1 Stand 12 silicone cupcake cases on a baking sheet or line a 12-section cupcake tin with paper or foil cake cases.

2 Melt the plain chocolate and the butter (see page 12), stirring frequently until smooth.

3 Put the eggs and sugar in a bowl and beat with a hand-held electric whisk or wooden spoon until light and creamy, then stir in the melted chocolate and butter. Sift the flour and baking powder into the bowl and gently fold them in with a large metal spoon.

4 Stir in the milk chocolate and nuts, then divide the cake mixture between the cases.

5 Bake in a preheated oven, 190°C (375°F), Gas Mark 5, for 12 minutes or until a crust has formed but the cakes feel quite soft underneath. Leave to cool in the tin for 10 minutes, then transfer to plates and top with small scoops of ice cream and a dusting of cocoa powder, if liked. Alternatively, serve cold.

malty raisin cupcakes

MAKES 12

PREPARATION TIME 10 MINUTES,
   PLUS STANDING

COOKING TIME 20 MINUTES

40 g (1½ oz) butter, cut into pieces
75 g (3 oz) bran flakes
225 ml (8 fl oz) milk
100 g (3½ oz) agave nectar or light muscovado
   sugar
125 g (4 oz) raisins
125 g (4 oz) self-raising flour
½ teaspoon baking powder

1 Stand 12 silicone cupcake cases on a baking sheet or line a 12-section cupcake tin with paper or foil cake cases.

2 Put the butter and bran flakes in a heatproof bowl. Bring the milk almost to the boil in a saucepan and pour into the bowl. Leave to stand for 10–15 minutes until the bran flakes are very soft and the mixture has cooled slightly, then stir in the agave nectar or sugar and the raisins.

3 Sift the flour and baking powder into the bowl and then stir until just mixed. Divide the cake mixture between the cases.

4 Bake in a preheated oven, 180°C (350°F), Gas Mark 4, for 20 minutes or until slightly risen and just firm to the touch. Transfer to a wire rack to cool.

jelly bean cupcakes

MAKES 12

PREPARATION TIME 20 MINUTES,
   PLUS COOLING AND SETTING

COOKING TIME 15–18 MINUTES

175 g (6 oz) butter
150 g (5 oz) caster sugar
2 eggs
1½ teaspoons vanilla extract
150 g (5 oz) plain flour
1½ teaspoons baking powder

FOR THE ICING AND DECORATION
125 g (4 oz) icing sugar, sifted
½ teaspoon vanilla extract
about 4 teaspoons water
a few drops of yellow food colouring, green
   food colouring and pink food colouring
selection of jelly beans, to decorate

1 Stand 12 silicone cupcake cases on a baking sheet or line a 12-section cupcake tin with paper or foil cake cases.

2 Put the butter, caster sugar, eggs and vanilla extract in a bowl, sift in the flour and baking powder and beat with a hand-held electric whisk or a wooden spoon until light and creamy. Divide the cake mixture between the cases.

3 Bake in a preheated oven, 180°C (350°F), Gas Mark 4, for 15–18 minutes or until well risen and just firm to the touch. Leave to cool in the tin.

4 Mix together the icing sugar, vanilla extract and enough water in a bowl to make a smooth icing. Divide the icing between 3 bowls and colour each batch with a different food colouring.

5 Remove the cakes from the tin, cover the tops with the different icings and decorate with jelly beans. Leave for 30 minutes for the icing to set.

sleepy
puppies

MAKES 12

PREPARATION TIME 45 MINUTES,
    PLUS COOLING

COOKING TIME 20 MINUTES

125 g (4 oz) butter, softened
125 g (4 oz) caster sugar
2 eggs
125 g (4 oz) self-raising flour
25 g (1 oz) cocoa powder
1/2 teaspoon baking powder

FOR THE BUTTERCREAM AND DECORATION

75 g (3 oz) unsalted butter, softened
125 g (4 oz) icing sugar, sifted, plus extra for
    dusting
a few drops of blue food colouring and black
    food colouring
300 g (10 oz) white ready-to-roll icing
25 g (1 oz) black ready-to-roll icing

1 Stand 12 silicone cupcake cases on a baking sheet or line a 12-section cupcake tin with paper or foil cake cases.

2 Put the butter, caster sugar and eggs in a bowl, sift in the flour, cocoa powder and baking powder and beat with a hand-held electric whisk or a wooden spoon until light and creamy. Divide the cake mixture between the cases.

3 Bake in a preheated oven, 180°C (350°F), Gas Mark 4, for 20 minutes or until risen and just firm to the touch. Transfer to a wire rack to cool.

4 Put the butter and icing sugar in a bowl and beat with a hand-held electric whisk or a wooden spoon until smooth and creamy. Beat in the blue food colouring and spread the buttercream over the cakes using a small palette knife.

5 Take 25 g (1 oz) of the white icing. Break off a little and reserve for the paws. Shape the remainder into a ball for the head, and flatten slightly. Cut the reserved icing in half and shape 2 paws. Position over the side of 1 cupcake. Position the head so that it overlaps the paws. Shape 2 floppy ears in black icing and secure to the head using a dampened paintbrush. Repeat for the remaining cakes.

6 Use the black food colouring and a fine paintbrush to paint a nose, mouth, eye, patch and claws on each pup.

blueberry & white chocolate cupcakes

MAKES 12

PREPARATION TIME 20 MINUTES

COOKING TIME 15 MINUTES

50 g (2 oz) butter, softened
150 g (5 oz) caster sugar
1 egg
150 g (5 oz) self-raising flour, sifted
100 ml (3½ fl oz) milk
1 teaspoon vanilla extract
100 g (3½ oz) blueberries
50 g (2 oz) white chocolate drops

FOR THE ICING

25 g (1 oz) blueberries, plus extra for decorating
4 tablespoons water
125 g (4 oz) icing sugar, sifted

1 Stand 12 silicone cupcake cases on a baking sheet or line a 12-section cupcake tin with paper or foil cake cases.

2 Put the butter and caster sugar in a bowl and beat with a hand-held electric whisk or a wooden spoon until light and creamy. Add the egg and flour and stir them in briefly, then add the remaining ingredients and stir them in quickly too. Divide the cake mixture between the cases.

3 Bake in a preheated oven, 190°C (375°F), Gas Mark 5, for 20 minutes or until risen and just firm to the touch. Transfer to a wire rack to cool.

4 Make the icing by placing a handful of the blueberries in a small saucepan with the water and heating gently on the hob. Mash the blueberries with the back of a wooden spoon until you have a bright purple mush, then remove from the heat and strain through a sieve or strainer into a small mixing bowl. Add the icing sugar and stir together to make a smooth, purple glacé icing. Drizzle the icing over the cupcakes, and place a nice fat blueberry on top of each one.

pirate faces

MAKES 12

PREPARATION TIME 45 MINUTES,
    PLUS COOLING

COOKING TIME 20 MINUTES

25 g (1 oz) unsalted butter, softened
50 g (2 oz) icing sugar, sifted, plus extra for
    dusting
a few drops of red food colouring
50 g (2 oz) green ready-to-roll icing
50 g (2 oz) white ready-to-roll icing
12 Vanilla Cupcakes (see page 16)
50 g (2 oz) black ready-to-roll icing
small foil-wrapped chocolate coins, to decorate
    (optional)

1 Put the butter and icing sugar in a bowl and beat with a hand-held electric whisk or a wooden spoon until light and creamy. Beat in the food colouring. Spoon the mixture into a piping bag fitted with a writing nozzle, or use a paper piping bag with the merest tip snipped off (see page 12).

2 Roll out the green icing on a worktop lightly dusted with icing sugar. Roll very thin ropes of white icing and position them about 5 mm (¼ inch) apart over the green icing. Roll gently with a rolling pin so that the ropes are flattened into the green icing to create a striped effect. Cut out little semicircular shapes and secure one to each cake to resemble a headscarf, using a little of the red buttercream. Use the icing trimmings to shape knots on 1 side.

3 Shape eyes and smiling mouths from white icing, and eye patches and pupils from black icing. Use the red buttercream in the bag to pipe wiggly lines for hair and around the mouths. Arrange on a plate, scattered with chocolate coins, if using.

orange & lemon cupcakes

MAKES 12

PREPARATION TIME 20 MINUTES,
PLUS COOLING AND SETTING

COOKING TIME 15–20 MINUTES

50 g (2 oz) butter, softened
100 g (3½ oz) caster sugar
2 eggs
100 g (3½ oz) self-raising flour, sifted
1 tablespoon finely grated lemon rind
2 tablespoons orange flower water
2–3 tablespoons milk

FOR THE ICING AND DECORATION
200 g (7 oz) icing sugar, sifted
1½ tablespoons orange juice
1½ tablespoons lemon juice
yellow food colouring and orange food
    colouring
finely pared orange rind and lemon rind coated
    in caster sugar, to decorate

1 Stand 12 silicone cupcake cases on a baking sheet or line a 12-section cupcake tin with paper or foil cake cases.

2 Put the butter, caster sugar, eggs, flour and grated lemon rind in a bowl and beat with a hand-held electric whisk or a wooden spoon until light and creamy. Add the orange flower water and enough milk to give a good dropping consistency. Divide the cake mixture between the cases.

3 Bake in a preheated oven, 200°C (400°F), Gas Mark 6, for 15–20 minutes or until risen and golden. Transfer to a wire rack to cool.

4 Slice the risen tops off the cakes. Mix half the icing sugar with the orange juice in 1 bowl and the other half with the lemon juice in another bowl. Dot a tiny amount of the relevant food colouring into each one and stir well until you have 2 pastel-coloured icings.

5 Pour a small amount of the orange icing over 6 of the cakes using a teaspoon to cover the surface evenly. Repeat with the remaining cakes, using the yellow icing. Decorate with the sugar-coated orange and lemon rind, pressing it on lightly. Leave to set completely.

coconut & raspberry cupcakes

MAKES 12

PREPARATION TIME 15 MINUTES

COOKING TIME 20 MINUTES

125 g (4 oz) butter
75 g (3 oz) self-raising flour
200 g (7 oz) icing sugar
50 g (2 oz) desiccated coconut
4 egg whites
200 g (7 oz) raspberries

1 Stand 12 silicone cupcake cases on a baking sheet or line a 12-section cupcake tin with paper or foil cake cases.

2 Put the butter in a small saucepan and melt over a low heat. Meanwhile, sift the flour and icing sugar into a large mixing bowl, add the coconut and stir together.

3 Add the egg whites and stir together, then add the melted butter and stir again until combined into a thick mixture. Tip the mixture into a measuring jug and divide it between the cases. Top with the raspberries

4 Bake in a preheated oven, 180°C (350°F), Gas Mark 4, for 20 minutes or until risen and just firm to the touch. Leave to cool in the tin for a few minutes before transferring them to a wire rack to cool completely.

chocolate peanut cupcakes

MAKES 12

PREPARATION TIME 25 MINUTES,
    PLUS COOLING AND SETTING

COOKING TIME 30 MINUTES

150 g (5 oz) butter, softened
150 g (5 oz) caster sugar
3 eggs
150 g (5 oz) self-raising flour
25 g (1 oz) cocoa powder
½ teaspoon baking powder

FOR THE CARAMEL AND ICING

75 g (3 oz) caster sugar
3 tablespoons water
75 ml (3 fl oz) double cream
25 g (1 oz) unsalted butter
50 g (2 oz) salted peanuts, finely chopped
100 g (3½ oz) plain chocolate, chopped
1 tablespoon golden syrup

1 Stand 12 silicone cupcake cases on a baking sheet or line a 12-section cupcake tin with paper or foil cake cases.

2 Put the butter, sugar and the eggs in a bowl, sift in the flour, cocoa powder and baking powder and beat with a hand-held electric whisk or a wooden spoon until light and creamy. Divide the cake mixture between the cases.

3 Bake in a preheated oven, 180°C (350°F), Gas Mark 4, for 20 minutes or until risen and just firm to the touch. Transfer to a wire rack to cool.

4 Put the sugar for the caramel in a small saucepan with the water and heat gently until the sugar has dissolved. Bring to the boil and boil rapidly for 4–5 minutes until the syrup has turned pale golden. Dip the base of the pan in cold water to prevent further cooking.

5 Add 50 ml (2 fl oz) of the cream and the unsalted butter to the syrup and heat very gently, stirring, to make a smooth caramel. Stir in the chopped nuts and leave until cool but not set. Spoon over the cupcakes.

6 Melt the chocolate with the remaining cream and golden syrup in a small saucepan over a gentle heat. Spoon over the cakes and leave to set.

fruity flower cupcakes

MAKES 12

PREPARATION TIME 30 MINUTES,
  PLUS COOLING

COOKING TIME 20 MINUTES

125 g (4 oz) butter, softened
125 g (4 oz) caster sugar
2 eggs
150 g (5 oz) self-raising flour
½ teaspoon baking powder
50 g (2 oz) semi-dried pineapple, finely chopped
4 tablespoons smooth apricot jam or red
  fruit jam
2 x 100 g (3½ oz) pots fruit-flavoured
  fromage frais
¼ small pineapple, peeled and cored
½ mango, stoned and peeled
3 raspberries, 3 blackberries 3 stoned cherries
  and 3 seedless black grapes, to decorate

1 Stand 12 silicone cupcake cases on a baking sheet or line a 12-section cupcake tin with paper or foil cake cases.

2 Put the butter, sugar and eggs in a bowl. Sift in the flour and baking powder and beat with a hand-held electric whisk or a wooden spoon until light and creamy. Divide the cake mixture between the cases and scatter with the semi-dried pineapple.

3 Bake in a preheated oven, 180°C (350°F), Gas Mark 4, for 20 minutes or until risen and just firm to the touch. Transfer to a wire rack to cool.

4 Spread each cake with a teaspoonful of the jam and then a thin layer of fromage frais. Slice the fresh pineapple and mango. Cut rounds from the fruit flesh using a 2.5 cm (1 inch) cutter and arrange about 5 in a circle over each cake to make a flower shape. Place a raspberry, blackberry, cherry or grape in the centre of each.

mud pies

MAKES 12

PREPARATION TIME 20 MINUTES

COOKING TIME 15 MINUTES

200 g (7 oz) dark chocolate, broken into
    small pieces
200 g (7 oz) butter
3 eggs
75 g (3 oz) caster sugar
100 g (3½ oz) self-raising flour, sifted
2 tablespoons cocoa powder or icing sugar,
    sifted, to decorate (optional)

1 Stand 12 silicone cupcake cases on a baking sheet or line a 12-section cupcake tin with paper or foil cake cases.

2 Put the chocolate and butter in a small heatproof bowl set over a pan of simmering water. Leave until melted, then stir together gently.

3 Put the eggs and sugar in a bowl and beat with a hand-held electric whisk for a full 5 minutes until very light and foamy. Add the flour and the melted chocolate mixture and fold them in gently with a large metal spoon. Divide the cake mixture between the cases.

4 Bake in a preheated oven, 160°C (325°F), Gas Mark 3, for 15 minutes or until risen and just firm to the touch. Leave to cool in the tin for 5–10 minutes before transferring to a wire rack. Sift the cocoa powder or icing sugar over the cakes to decorate, if wanted.

pumpkin heads

MAKES 12

PREPARATION TIME 30 MINUTES

COOKING TIME 10–15 MINUTES

100 g (3½ oz) butter, softened
100 g (3½ oz) caster sugar
a few drops of vanilla extract
2 eggs
100g (3½ oz) self-raising flour, sifted

FOR THE DECORATION

1 pack ready-to-roll coloured icing (contains
    4 x 125 g (4 oz) packs in red, yellow, green
    and black)
black icing pen (optional)

1 Stand 12 silicone cupcake cases on a baking sheet or line a 12-section cupcake tin with paper or foil cake cases.

2 Put the butter, sugar and vanilla extract in a bowl and beat with a hand-held electric whisk or a wooden spoon until light and creamy. Add the eggs and beat the mixture again, then add the flour and gently fold it in with a large metal spoon. Divide the cake mixture between the cases.

3 Bake in a preheated oven, 180°C (350°F), Gas Mark 4, for 10–15 minutes or until risen and golden. Allow to cool for a few minutes before transferring to a wire rack to cool completely.

4 Knead the red and the yellow icings together to form orange. Pinch off a little piece of the green icing and shape into a ball, then flatten into a circle and gently push on to the top of a cake. Pinch off a bigger piece of the orange icing and roll it into a ball. Place this on top of the green 'pumpkin patch'. Now pinch a tiny piece of green and roll it into a stalk and push it on to the top of the orange pumpkin. Also take tiny pinches of the black and use to make eyes and a crooked smile. Alternatively, draw the face on to the pumpkin head with a black icing pen.

little devil cupcakes

MAKES 12

PREPARATION TIME 15 MINUTES

COOKING TIME 10–15 MINUTES

100 g (3½ oz) butter, softened
100 g (3½ oz) caster sugar
a few drops of vanilla extract
2 eggs
100 g (3½ oz) self-raising flour
3 tablespoons cocoa powder

FOR THE ICING AND DECORATION

2 packs (250 g/18 oz) ready-made red fondant
   icing, to decorate
1 tablespoon preboiled warm water

1 Stand 12 silicone cupcake cases on a baking sheet or line a 12-section cupcake tin with paper or foil cake cases.

2 Put the butter, sugar and vanilla extract in a bowl and beat with a hand-held electric whisk or a wooden spoon until light and creamy. Add the eggs, beating after each addition, then sift in the flour and cocoa powder and gently fold them in with a large metal spoon. Divide the cake mixture between the cases.

3 Bake in a preheated oven, 180°C (350°F), Gas Mark 4, for 20 minutes or until risen and firm to the touch. Leave to cool for a few minutes before transferring to a wire rack to cool completely.

4 Put 1½ packs of the fondant icing in a bowl, add the water and stir until you have a thick but spreadable icing. When the cakes are cool, spread the icing over the tops with the back of a teaspoon or with a palette knife.

5 Roll small pieces of the remaining fondant icing into devil's horns, then stick them into the wet icing on top of the cakes.

easter nests

MAKES 12

PREPARATION TIME 20 MINUTES

COOKING TIME 15 MINUTES

75 g (3 oz) butter
50 g (2 oz) soft light brown sugar
1 tablespoon golden syrup or honey
125 g (4 oz) porridge oats
mini sugar-coated chocolate eggs, to decorate

1 Stand 12 silicone cupcake cases on a baking sheet or line a 12-section cupcake tin with paper or foil cake cases.

2 Put the butter, sugar and golden syrup into a large saucepan over a gentle heat and stir until melted together and just starting to bubble. Remove the pan from the heat and add the oats, then stir together until they are evenly covered. Divide the mixture between the cases.

3 Bake in a preheated oven, 180°C (350°F), Gas Mark 4, for 20 minutes or until risen and just firm to the touch. Make a dip in the middle of each nest with the tip of a teaspoon so that they look like little nests, then leave to cool on a wire rack.

4 Put a few mini eggs into each nest to decorate, then peel off the cases to serve.

ducks,
bunnies
& chicks

MAKES 12

PREPARATION TIME 35 MINUTES,
  PLUS COOLING

COOKING TIME 20 MINUTES

1 quantity Buttercream (see page 14)
a few drops of yellow food colouring and blue
  food colouring
12 Vanilla Cupcakes (see page 16)
2 glacé cherries

1 Put two-thirds of the buttercream in a bowl and beat in the yellow food colouring. Spread the buttercream in a flat layer over the tops of the cooled cakes using a small palette knife.

2 Colour the remaining buttercream with the blue food colouring. Put in a piping bag fitted with a writing nozzle, or use a paper piping bag with the merest tip snipped off (see page 12).

3 Pipe simple duck, bunny and chick shapes on to the buttercream-topped cakes. Cut the glacé cherries into very thin slices and then into tiny triangles. Use to represent beaks on the ducks and chicks, and tiny eyes on the bunnies.

index

acknowledgements

Executive Editor Eleanor Maxfield
Managing Editor Clare Churly
Executive Art Editor Penny Stock
Designer Ashley Western
Picture Library Manager Jennifer Veall
Production Controller Linda Parry

Photography: Octopus Publishing Group/Stephen Conroy 39; /Vanessa Davies 6 top, 6 bottom, 7 top, 7 bottom, 13 right, 19, 20, 25, 29, 32, 42, 49, 54, 57, 59, 60; /David Munns 8 left, 8 right, 11, 12, 13 left, 15, 16, 23, 26, 31, 35, 36, 41, 45, 50, 53; /Lis Parsons 46; /Gareth Sambidge 63. Cover: Octopus Publishing Group/Vanessa Davies